This Beautiful Chaos Life

Danielle Saeland

BookLeaf Publishing

India | USA | UK

Presentation by *BookLeaf Publishing*

Web: www.bookleafpub.com

E-mail: info@bookleafpub.com

ISBN: 9789363314832

First edition 2024

I dedicate this book-

To: my best friend, my soul mate, my everything..my husband.

To: The tiny-crazy-but-absolutely-beautiful raiders..we created together-our children..

Mira Victoria, Layla Sofia & Kevin Brett III.

To: my Mother, my Father, my Step-mother, my Sister, my Niece & my Nephew.

Without ALL of your guidance, wisdom,

advice, support and unconditional love..

MY inner LIGHT would have NEVER became so bright.

I am everything..I am..because of ALL of YOU.

I am so GRATEFUL and BLESSED to have all of you in my life!

May this book bring you JOY, HAPPINESS and fill your hearts with UNCONDITIONAL LOVE, like you have shown me.

May this book be your INSPIRATION.

May it bring at YOUR LIGHT.

May it HELP you-

SHINE brighter, than EVER before.

This one-this book-is for all of you!

Love,

Dani

And last but not least-

My Spirit Guides & my Guardian Angels-

Thank you for my dreams..

ACKNOWLEDGEMENT

Thank you BookLeaf Publishing for this opportunity to write for 21 days.
This challenge alone-has made me write again!
It gave me just the push I needed..
to reach out of my comfort zone..to reach just a littler higher in myself!
It helped bring back my inner light! Thank you!

Thank you to every single person in my life.
Especially, my husband, my 3 amazing babies..my mom, my dad, my step-mom, my sister, my niece & my nephew.

Just the love you have for me-the unconditional love & support-has fueled me to be a better person.
I love you all with every ounce of my soul.
Thank you!
Never stop being you!

Danielle

PREFACE

This is my very 1st book-ever!!
I feel so special.. honored..that you are reading
this today!

It's been a dream of mine-to some day-have my
writings out in the world-for all to read..
Thank you! My heart & soul are shining brighter
today..because of you!

I have always loved writing.. poems &
stories..anything.. It just comes natural to me. I
can put words on paper, better than I can through
talking.
When I was younger- in my pre-teens-I wrote A
LOT. Then life happened and I just stopped..
I fell in love, got married, had 3 incredible
beautiful babies.. things got crazy!!
During the massive jungle it is to be a mom-hold
a job, run a house, homeschool & finding
yourself again in the mix-
I found a different creative outlet-painting!
I started painting what I saw in my dreams..
stars, mountains..universes.. the love for
painting just grew & grew..

Teaching my 3 babies to not only paint but, to be free with art, is one of my greatest blessings in my life!!

Then one day-when cleaning out my closet-I found my old writings from my childhood. After reading all my collections I wrote so long ago..It sparked something inside me so deep.
It opened up my mind, heart & soul to start writing again..
I 'felt' I could write again..
Within a few weeks after that, I can across the 21 day writing challenge.
(This challenge was to write a poem-each day for 21 days- then submit it to BookLeaf Publishing, then they will help publish it)
I thought to myself.. 'Can I do that?' '
'It's a huge challenge..' '
'Can I even write that much?'..
'But just maybe..maybe it is just the challenge I need to REALLY let it out!'
So I paid the small fee & joined.
These 21 days have had LOTS of ups & downs.
Good days & bad days.. but each day-I gave it my all-and wrote..
Because..what do I got to loose??
So..this book-these writings-are what come out..
I hope these writings bring you
joy..happiness..maybe even sadness..I hope

maybe..it inspires you.. just one person..to
'Start-Again'.. there's never a better time..then
now!
Let your light shine!

Danielle

*If your interested in our artwork you can check
us out here:
https://www.foundmyself.com/ThisBeautifulCha
osLife
*Feel free to look around, email us, like,
comment, chat-absolutely zero pressure to
purchase anything-we just love the likes &
comments!
email: ThisBeautifulChasoLife@gmail.com

Just do Art.. in this..Beautiful Chaos Life

I've always been creative, messy &
all over the place-since I can remember..
always only, engaged in art.
Anything art.
But my new recent love..
Paint.
I love to paint.
My mind stops racing..
My heart slows down..
My hand is one with the brush.
Colors blending together..
Dark to light..
Lighter to darker..
It soothes my soul.
I'm at peace.
My happy place.
My art is messy.
Creative. But colorful.
Dark & night skies..
Stars.. lots of stars..
Moons, mountains, everywhere..
Everywhere in my dreams..
and in every universe I fly to-
In my dreams..

Then there's my babies..
My ultimate..happy place & love.
Star seeds blossoming into true form..
Messy artists & paint splatters..
But smiles & giggles for days..
Memory making in progress..
A life of love and everything art.
My oldest of gracious heart.
An animal soul with a spirit of a horse..
Compassion & love for all.
A dark hair miracle.
My middle is my lion.
Leo is brave, loyal &
Loving..Devoted…
Beautiful & kind.
My son..
Wild & free.
Cuddly & sweet..
Bold.
Charming. And..
A boy!
But I wouldn't want it any other way.
Messy.
Creative.
All over the place.
All the time.
Always moving..
Then there is you..
My other half.

My soul mate.
Connected by chance,
But brought together by the stars..
glowing in the moonlight and
Dancing in the sun.
Our life is so messy..
All over the place.
But with you,
It's more of an
Adventure!
You lift me up!
Never break me down..
You help me grow…help me to get
Out of my comfort zone.
You help..find 'us'.
All five of us.
In..
This beautiful Chaos life..
and I wouldn't want it with anyone else-
But you.

Just do art..
In this..
Beautiful Chaos
Life.

My bull, My lion, My balance

With magic from above-
Unexpected, but deeply loved,
In the month of May, a miracle, she came.
She brought joy, hope and light
-just like her name.
A soul of animal spirit. So wild and free.
Her existence is almost enchanting to me.
Three years later, god gave her a sister.
In the hottest summer known to man-
After the sparks of fireworks-it was gods plan.
In the month of July, the angel of night, she was
known.
This Leo, of beauty, class and a little sass,
A dynamic personality of all her own.
A fierce lion. And one heck of a roar!
So logical, so strong. So stubborn and beautiful.
So courageous. So determined. This girl brought
so much more!
So perfect, this little sister, to much adore.
Her presence of grace. Her existence-
in this world, has a wonderful place.
Fast forward, three years more.
These two baby girls, soon greeted a Mr.
With the changing leaves, and colors of fall-

Near the scariest holiday of all.
In the month of October, a boy was born. Boo!
God sent a brother to those two.
A little prince, to add to the palace.
Bringing with him, a sense of balance.
And like his name-handsome- it's true.
In that rocking chair, mommy's boo.
Sweet. charming. Full of life and on the go.
Touch this, grab that, climb this, push that.
Always going with the flow.
My bull, my lion, my balance.
My babies, forever you'll be.
You three-promise me,
Will do wonders in this world.
You will see, its fate.
Someday, just wait.
My bull.
My lion.
My balance.
My babies, forever-
You, will be.

Written in the Stars

When the day comes to an end..
And the sun starts to set..
The darkness will start to creep in..
But have no worry, fear or doubt..

For one by one, as they start to trickle in..
They begin to bring the light.
They, together, turn the night sky ever so bright.
Soon the whole sky is filled with them..
Those small, yet so beautiful little things..
Those Twinkling little stars..
And with them, the darkness is once more-
Not so dark.
The same goes for our love & life together..
Just as the stars in the night sky will always
shine..
Our love will always do the same..
Because, love..
Our love, will always shine.

So on a clear night,
When all the stars take shape..
Look for that tiny constellation..
You know the one..
Not the Big Dipper, and not the small one..

But the one that we first saw together..
Remember that one?

'The shopping cart'.
That tiny group of light.
Made of just a few stars..
Was our beginning.
But little did we know..
It is also the heart of Taurus..
That just so happened by surprise..
To be our first born child.
To the left of that gentle bull,
Stands strong and proud..
The hunter.
Your favorite constellation..
Orion.
With his bright shining belt
And bow above..
you will find it.
Our whole life story..
Shining bright as ever..
'This Beautiful Chaos Life'
Is its name.

So, when your having a bad day..
Or on the nights that your up late..
Just look up to find that light..
The light of our life together.
For those constellations..

For they shine bright for you..
Forever.
Forever and always.
Just like our love..
And our chaos life..
But so beautiful..
In so many ways..
It will never stop shining.

I hope it brings you joy, happiness
And a smile to your soul..
To know,
'This beautiful chaos life'
Will always shine bright for you.
Now, and for always.
So where ever you are-
Where ever you go-
It will always be there.
In your heart, in your soul..
And now in the stars..
For it is now..
Officially..
Written in the stars..
And not just for a thousand lifetimes but,
Till the end of time.

Beautiful Badass

I am grateful. I am hopeful.
I am happy. I am joyful.
I am wealthy. I am generous.
I am spiritual. I am a dreamer.
I am a teacher. I am a healer.
I am creative. I am an artist.
I am a writer. I am a story teller.
I am the moon. I am the stars.
I am the universe.
I am loved. I am beautiful.
I am a
Beautiful Badass.

Raiders of my Ship

Massive destruction!!
Breaking and smashing!!
Complete chaos!!!
Most days-It's like a shipwreck…
But so Wild and free..
Fearless but never forgetful!!
Always asking after a maybe…
Can, we, can we?! Pretty please!!
Every question 10x & more.
Adventurous little creatures..
Look at me!! look at me!!
Mighty thief's they are!
Day & night-be ware!
Breakfast..snack..lunch..snack..dinner..
but I'm not hungry!!!!
Can I have a snack?
To the kitchen..we raid!!
Get ready for bed. No!
We cant go to sleep!
Not yet! No bed, we say!!
PJ's. Brush teeth.
Sword fight, we must!
Into bed now please. No way!
But..can I have a snack?
Just one bite??

Why so much mutiny??? I say!
Goodnight my little pirates!
But..mom…?!!!
Hand over your swords, I say..At once!!
Close your eyes my little raiders..
Sleep tight!!
Because tonight-
This mom- is taking back this ship!
Now fight!!

I'm in Love

I'm in love with the moon-
The sun & all the shining stars.
I'm in love with a bull, a lion and the balancing
act..
I'm in love with a twin of me.
I'm in love with the mountains, the woods, the
oceans & the starry night skies.
I'm in love with all the crazy adventures & the
quiet long nights.
I'm in love with the late night conversations
& the sleepy hours.
I'm in love with movie nights & the family
game nights.
I'm in love with my family.
I'm in love with the blanket snuggles & the
goodnight kisses.
I'm in love with the messy paint splatters & the
little artists in making.
I'm in love with the art work, all scattered about.
I'm in love with the endless dreams told when
the fire is burning.
I'm in love with the smell of rain.
I'm in love with the changing of seasons.
I am in love with my dreams & the ability to fly.
I'm in love with my angels, sent from above.

I'm in love with you.
I'm in love with your hopes & dreams.
I'm in love with how together-we conquer.
I'm in love with this life with you.
I'm so in love.
With you.

Colors from her soul

For as long as I can remember,
I have been walking in a fog.
A foggy kind of storm..
Chaos.
It was only ever filled with-
Swirling shades of gray.
I could only ever see distorted shapes.
I could never see,
truly see, inside of it.

One day, just like every other day-
A brilliant flash caught my eye.
Was it just another mirage or mind trick?
I thought to myself.
There it was again.
And again.

So, I began to look closer.
And closer..
When I got close enough to see..
To really see..
I saw her.
A girl.
Just standing there..
Calm inside this chaos storm.

She didn't seem to be searching for anything..
No, instead..
She held a single brush.
And she was just painting..
I asked with astonishment..
'Where are all the colors?'
She said softly, without looking at me..
'I don't need them..
This brush brings all the colors I need.
They come from my soul..'

She gracefully moved her body
with each brush stroke..
Almost as if, her paintings moved her.
I then asked the girl,
If I could follow her.
She turned her head slowly to look at me,
And said softly..
'Yes'.
As our eyes locked,
I saw something..
Something that could only be described as..
Magic.
The girl was always looking forward
And moving to her own brush strokes..
She looked so amazed at her own colors.
Her beautiful painted chaos.

I tripped.
Then looked back.
I expected to see the gray foggy storm.
But what I saw instead..
This time..
Was more like a work of art.
I saw it this time-
With the colors she gave it.
I could see beauty..

The paintings she did with that brush..
-The spots where she dripped paint-
Even those chaos parts,
I could see meaning beyond words.

I no longer saw a foggy gray storm..
For I could finally see it.
A beautiful life.
A beautiful life that had to be painted..
by a girl..
A girl with magic in her eyes
And a single paint brush,
That gave her all the colors she needed..
All the colors..
From her soul.

By: K2

Who am I, really?

I am a day dreamer.
A star gazer.
I am a sunset watcher..
I am a beach walker.
I am a treasure finder.
A rock collector.
I am an artist.
A painter, a writer.
I am a daughter. A sister.
A wife, a mother.
A forever friend.
A cook, a teacher, a boo-boo fixer..
A lover, a soul connection.
I am a nature lover.
Trees, wildflowers and rivers..
I am a cat lover. A dirt bike rider..
I am a quote believer.
An inspirational seeker.
I am a, let my spirits guide me..
Let my angels carry me.
I am on a spiritual journey..
A endless soul experience.
I am thoughts of manifestation.
I am a grateful heart,
A forgiving mind..

In a beautiful body.
But who am I really?
For, I am-
My own creator.

This Chaos Life

Dirty hands. I swear.
Messy hair. We don't care!
Torn clothes. Mismatched socks.
Messes everywhere. Nothing clean!
Dishes stacked. Laundry scattered.
Cats everywhere. A forever animal zoo!
Tiny raiders yelling. Adults swearing!
Sleep in. Stay up late. Never enough sleep.
To the beach! To the mountains! Random drives
to nowhere. Sight-seeing, so freeing.
Sometimes early. Sometimes late.
No empty bellies. Pantry full.
Do I even know today's date?
Game night with music.
Movie night with popcorn.
Cuddles on the couch.
Bath time with bubbles.
Warm hugs & cozy blanket snuggles.
Quads. Bicycles. Motorcycles. Scooters.
Helmets and googles. Knee pads?
Yeah right. Band-aides and bruised knees.
Monkey bars and slides.
Skate parks and swings.
Can we go? Pretty please?!
Grandpas house. To the woods!

Cabin making, tree tipping & hose water
sipping. Dirt trails and Deer.
Riding around town in 1st gear.
Long drives. Short walks.
Rivers and creeks..Paths and roads..
Where are we going? Nobody knows!
Day drives. Weekend trips.
Camping in the desert. Tent sleeping.
Road trip for weeks. There's so much to see!
Hop cities! Jump states!
Truck sleeping..not for me!
Coast to desert. Valleys and sunsets.
Canyons to craters.. and..Aliens, oh my!
No shower. Maybe a toilet?
Maybe the side of the road..
Anyone have TP?
Home again. Unpack. Wash clothes.
Mom! There's no food! Shopping..again.
Stomach aches and head aches.
Don't forget the trip to bend!
Or the sleepover over with cousins,
next weekend!
Full calendar. No rest.
Next, Bowling! Arcades! Go karts! Mini golf!
I want the blue car! No, I do! No fair!
Play this game, and that one.
Don't forget the crane!
Win prizes with tokens.
Mom is pulling out her hair!!

Pizza. Mac n cheese. Pb&J's. No crust.
Is it nap time yet?
Yeah right!! no bed time set..
Mom! It's raining, where am my boots?
Mud puddles. Hoodies, umbrellas.
I'm wet. I'm cold. Where's the fire??
Kids!!..we need wood. Use the dryer.
'Uhh..why do we have to do everything?!?!'
Rock collecting..Stick carrying..
Oh look!..another wildflower!
Ice cream, popsicles..Oh no!!! more sugar!
Blowing bubbles & Birthdays candles.
Sun burns & tans. Where's the fan???
Fire pit. Everything burning.
Stories during smores. Fireworks on the 4th.
Constellations, Orion & Leo.
Look!! I just saw a shooting star!
Slip n slides. Sprinkles. Can we have a pool?
Climbing trees. Putting up hammocks.
Mow grass. Chop weeds.
In winter, sleds & snowmen.
Scarfs & gloves. Now it's spring!!
No.. wait. Winter. Again. More snow. Oh, no…
Hot chocolate in your favorite mug.
Stack wood. Keep the stove burning!
Santa lists & stockings. Decorations. Drive by
lights. Milkshake & fries.
It's time to read a book!!!
Write a story, a note. ABCs & 123s..

Can we make art?
Canvas. Brushes. And the occasional-paint splatters!!
Crafts & DIY's. Coloring books & markers.
Crayons & pencils.
Little artists at heart!!
Building blanket forts for hours…
And mom stepping over lego towers!!
Calling friends & sending post cards.
Picture taking & photo printing.
Wiping tears & ending fights.
Bed time stores & goodnight kisses..
'I forgot..there's no clean dishes!!!'

The love & the Light

The light in my heart,
That comes from only art.
The love in my soul.
So colorful, never dull.
I pray to my angels, my guides,
Forever, by my side.
In my heart, my light shines
To my soul, it binds.
In my dreams, I fly,
Through the starry night sky.
To universes, and back
Always alone, never in a pack.
My soul is of love-
Like a Noah's ark dove.
My mind feels at peace
My body, never decease.
Connected by grace,
A forever star chase.
The light in my heart
A bright shine, never apart
The love in my soul
For all, it has total control.

I.AM.GROOT

I love baby groot. He is a tree..
I love trees!
My favorite number is 5, because I am 5.
I like the letter K. My name is Kevin and
Kevi..and Mommy's boo butt.
'HAHAHAHA!!!' I said, BUTT! 'HAHA!!'
My favorite person, is my mommy. And daddy
too.
I -kinda- like my sisters..Sometimes..
Mostly, I like Cam & Kay. They are my cousins.
And my best friends too!
I am the youngest, of the cousin crew.
But.. also, the loudest! What?!
'I CANT HELP IT!!! Hahahaha!!
I like to be loud. Never quiet. I like to move!
I like to bounce around, off the walls -like a
crazy person- I like to jump, and push, and
pull..and punch my sisters..
(Shh.. don't tell mom..)
oh, and climb! I like climbing things!
My favorite foods are= PB&J's. NO CRUST!
And..CHEESE pizza!! Pizza schimza cheese
pizza!!
My favorite things to do:

Wrestle & fight with daddy. Play tag. Play with
my dump trucks. Play with my tow truck. Eat ice
cream. Watch the trash truck. Go up & down the
slides at parks. Eat food.
Annoy my sisters..
My favorite color is red. Like my mommy's!
My favorite super hero is baby groot.
I like groot.
My favorite movies are ones with baby groot in
them. Oh and 'home alone' KEVIN!!'
..but definitely NOT titanic!
I like turtles. I like dogs & cats. I like food..
I like to push food away from me at the table..
when it's gross!! Broccoli!? Yuck!
Salad? No way!! I'll push it off!!
I want to buy a toy dragon.
I like Halloween -except that one year-
Where that guy scared me!!
I like fireworks! More! More! More!!
I like stars. The shooting kind.
So I can make a wish..for that toy dragon!
I like snow! Mainly, because.. I like to throw
snowballs at people.. so they can freeze to
death!! Hahaha!! Just kidding, mom!
Mom says the only time I'm quiet is when I'm
sleeping..
Nope! Not me!!
I snore. And I squirm! Never quiet!
Oh, and I like dinosaurs.

That's it.
End of my poem..

By: K3 age 5

P/S
Will trade my sisters for a dinosaur!

Shortcuts

Do not take shortcuts-
Take the scenic route..
it is much more beautiful.
It may take longer-
Then the highway.
You should still go..the long way..
It's much more beautiful.
And much more..
Enchanting & crazy..
And just-
Wonderful.

By: Mira Saeland age 12

Follow your Dreams

Trust your spirit & never take a shortcut in life.
Take the long route because you pick up more
experiences on the way.
Live life to its fullest. Never give up on your
dreams.
Even if it seems that your dreams are
impossible..
Don't let this crazy world push you around &
take you away from those dreams.
Your dreams are who you are.
You could always find new dreams-
If you take the long route.

By: Kaylynn Brewster age 13

Create

Dreams are who you are-
Like rocks & crystals.
Let your dreams cover you-
Like the beautiful sunset in the sky.
Let dreams guide you-
Like a horse with no lead.
Create your dreams with paint-
In this beautiful world.

By: Layla age 8

The land where Angels live

As far back as I can recall..
They were there- in my dreams.
Whenever I needed them, I could call.
They patched all my broken seams.
When I could no longer- even crawl..
They picked me up & carried me,
Through my sleepy eyes, I could see..
Places from another world.
Their whispers- almost swirled.
For so many years,
Through so many tears-
These angels- my guides
My answers- they provide.
Gratitude to them, I give-
To the land where my
Angels live.

Beautiful Soul

Right from the start,
you could see..
Right through my walls
Almost, as if I had none.
Your dark eyes, almost shimmering..
Shined straight to my soul.
My heart knew-
But my brain fought it..
What is this? I thought..
Just by one look. Just by one stare..
I let you in.
You brought out my light-
That was hidden for so long.
I spent years to build my walls.
But you. But with you..
It only took just a second.
My brick wall had no purpose.
My heart lite up from the inside.
My soul 'felt'..
It was a new feeling.
I didn't know what to do with it.
Do I continue running?
Like I always did..
But I didn't want to.
I wanted to stay.

I wanted to be right next to you.
Forever.
It was like a tether-
or like a single missing puzzle piece-
I was missing..
Standing by your side..
I felt the world. I felt I 'could'.. do anything!
Yes-at first-it was a hurricane..
Spinning and swirling..
But then it became, magic.
Like under a spell..
Mixed with all the good.. for once.
Joy. Excitement. Happiness.
Love.
Purpose.
Still a wirlwind of chaos..
But it's so beautiful.
You're so beautiful.
Your soul and mine..
What a
Beautiful chaos.
Life.
What a
Beautiful soul
You.
Are.

LORD

Oh lord, please be my guide-
Please provide me with strength-
Help me overcome challenges I may face. Help
me stay strong-
In my journey here on earth.
Oh lord, please provide me with laughter-
Help the playful child inside my heart-come
back to life-Help me..come back to life.
Oh, lord please be my guide-
Oh, lord please provide me with sadness-
With no tears to run down my cheek,
I may never feel joy.
Oh, lord, please help me find all that I seek..
Oh lord, please be my guide.
Oh, lord please provide me with patience-
Help me take each new day with delight. Help
me to appreciate the little things. Please help me
to learn how to slow down.
Oh, lord please be my guide-
Please provide me with dedication-
Help me hold on to my faith. Help me find my
true purpose, my calling.
Help me to continue to move forward, even on
the days, I feel I can't.
Oh lord, please be my guide-

Oh, lord please provide me with your light-
Help me overcome the darkness.
Help me find my light. Help me to ignite the
light in others. Help me learn to serve the world
through your light.
Oh, lord please provide me with love-
That real, raw, unconditional love.
To feel passion, compassion & hope for all.
Oh, lord, please be my guide-
Oh lord please provide me with your presence &
your grace-
Help me to understand that you are always near.
Please guide me in my thoughts & in my dreams
with your words.
Please guide me with your angels-
But most of all, oh lord,
Please provide me with gratitude-
Help me appreciate. Help me give thanks. Help
me show it to all the animals, big & small. To all
the people, bad & good.
To all magnificent beauty you have placed
before me. To all that was created by your touch.
To all in this universe..
Help me to grow. Help me to understand. Help
me learn. Help me feel truly blessed for always..
Oh, lord-
Please be my guide.
Amen.

What hurts the most-

What hurts the most-
That you're contacting me really at all.
Yeah, txt here and there..
But when's the last time I heard your voice?
Days ago..
It's killing me.
I played that video I took of you-
The one of you, reading poetry to me.
Over and over and over again.
Just to hear your voice.
You're my best friend. My partner.
My husband.
Yeah, I know, I told you to go.
I told you to go spend time with your family.
But not even a phone call every now and then?
That before you go to bed?
I can't help but wonder..
Is it really my heart your wanting?
Is it really our future you hope for?
Is it really our life together that you desire?
I'm thinking the worst with not hearing from
you.
I want you to find yourself again.
Be better.
For you.

And for us.
But do you want us?
Do you want this family you have with us?
Or do you want something else?
I've told you before and I'll say it again-
I'd rather you be happy somewhere else
Then in misery with me.
But at least talk to me.
It's been 12 years.
12 years with you by my side.
How long have we actually gone not speaking to
each other?
How did that go?
Yeah, we had problems in the past..
A lot of ups and downs..
But we rarely ever..
Went without speaking.
It's what hurts the most right now.
How are you?
What are you up to?
Anything fun and interesting?
I want to be the first person you tell all your
stories to! But am I?
I have so much to tell you since you left!
I feel like we are drifting even further apart..
Are we? Are you?
I trust you with everything I have.
You have always had my heart.
Every piece of it.

But that also means-
You're the only one that can make my heart hurt
it so bad.
What do you want in life? In your future?
Your dreams? Hopes? Desires?
Can you tell me?
Do you want to tell me?
I don't want to live without you.
But it's more than that.
I want to live with you by my side.
Till the lord takes us away-together..
All my dreams, hopes and desires are with
YOU!
I hope you're doing ok.
I just wanted to say-
It's what hurts the most-
Today..

The Manual

*I am not easy to deal with. At all. Believe me, I'm fully 1000% aware.
*I am complicated. Like to the max level.
*I am boring.. to most. But not to me!
*I don't know how to start most conversations especially-when trying to process new information or in a social setting.
*I am not a very emotional person. But really, I am full of emotions. I just don't show it very well..I'm working on that, I promise!
*'Bitch face' is my 'normal' face. It ruin's a lot of my relationships but I don't want it to. I'm working on that to..
*If I cry, then I am sad. Sometimes I happy cry, again, complicated.
*I don't know how to deal with myself-let alone other females. I get alone with males better, always have.
*I don't make friends easy, at all.
* Honestly, 'friends' can & will slow me down. However, that DOESN'T mean I don't want friends..I just don't trust easy..
* I actually LOVE alone time. I thrive on it. It's my re-charge time.

*I, 99% of the time do what is asked of me. It may take me hours, days, weeks or more-to process and execute said thing.

*If I make a promise or say, 'I will' or 'I do', I will do it. 100% of the time. Give me time.

* Sometimes you have to remind me of that promise. I DID NOT forget about it. The tab is still open in my brain.

* By the way, I have a 'special power' in my brain that is on hyper drive, ALL THE TIME.

* I do not speak well with words through my mouth but words through my writing is my soul speaking.

* Read my writings. They hold my inner thoughts.

* A paint brush in my hand, holds power.

* I, 99% of the time, have no idea what I'm doing. I do this thing..it's called 'wing'n it'.

* You may or may not want to follow my lead. I'm NOT a leader or a boss. But I am a teacher, coach, mentor..all in one.

* I am currently on a 'finding my life path/purpose' journey. Hold on, it gets wild!

* I don't want to ask for help, so knowing when to ask for help, is so freaking hard for me! Please help!

* I want to do everything myself, all at once or nothing at all. It's my nature. Gemini here, sorry, not sorry.

* I just 'know' a great deal of 'things'. I can't
explain it. It just is.
* I am a dreamer. Day-dreamer, night dreamer,
travel-in-my-sleep dreamer.
* I can talk to my spirit guides & guardian
angels. I have several of them. I can also
Astro-travel. I've been able to do this for a
VERY long time. Just ask!
* I can ask them a question & get an answer
fairly quickly. I HAVE to listen to them. Can't
explain that, it just is.
* I have seen & been to, many different
universes & timelines. And I paint what I see.
* I am a quiet & reserved person but also an
open book. Ask me any question. Yup, you have
to ask me. I WONT start the conversation..
* I absolutely LOVE deep conversations.
Conspiracies, crazy theories, aliens, the sun, the
stars, spirituality..
* I need intelligent before anything else. No
'real' conversation, then I get bored. It happens
fast, so watch out.
* When I say something, then don't talk about it
for a time, nothing has changed since the last
time I talked about it.
* When I'm silent, it doesn't mean I'm mad or
upset, it means I'm processing information.
*That 'super power', has a million tabs open in

my brain at once, it works like a computer.
'Processing power' sometimes slows it down.
* Sometimes, my computer brain needs a
'restart' or gets 'over-loaded' and a 'freeze'
happens..which probably means..
* I need space. A lot. Remember, I THRIVE on
alone time. 'Re-charge' time.
* I need this time more than I actually want.
Sometimes I want space but want your company.
And probably 99% of the time, I don't even
know which one I need or want. Again, I'm
complicated.
* If you ask me what I want or need & I reply,
make sure to ask again. Clarify it. Give me a few
minutes to respond. Then respond with what I
say.
* I don't mean to have excuses. For nearly
everything.. it's a trauma response. I'm working
it..
* I've learned in just the last few months- I have
lived in 'survival' mode for A VERY LONG
time. Trying to un-tangle that..
* I am a human and I am working on trying to
better myself, every day. Be gentle & kind.
*I have been labeled a 'bitch' most of my life. I
totally get it however, if you don't like
something I say or do..please tell me. I can't
change it if I don't know about it. I do know
now, that I am no longer fueled' by rage.

* I was in pain most of my life. Since about age 10 to 34 years old. It made me angry and that mixed with a lot of unhealed traumas- turned into rage. I am TRULY sorry if that EVER came out to you. I DID NOT mean it. I am sorry..
* I live on quotes, affirmations, inspirational words.. they speak volume to my soul.
* My self talk is HUGE. Don't interrupt it.
* I am also a very deep, deep, passionate, 'spiritual being' in a human body just trying to navigate this world. Work with me.
*When I love. I LOVE. I love with all my heart and soul.
* When I have a friend or am a friend to others-it's for life. A forever bond. Until that friend destroys the relationship regardless of what I want or not.
* I have many walls up around my heart for a reason. But if you dare to peek behind them, the talks we can have!! But you may think I'm insane, I'm use to it..
* I can 'research' like no one's business. I soak up information like a sponge, as long as I like the topic. If I don't, forget about it..
* 99% of the time, I want friends. I want to be around people.
* I need people to lean on, talk to, be around, hangout with, but my boring-ness or 'bitch face/bitchness' is too much for 99% of people.

Again, it ruins relationships & I'm working on
it.
* When I talk, it's important. You should listen.
* I am an introvert, a 1,000%. but also a
'projector'. If giving the right people- & if my
information is wanted- I can help guide you on
whatever journey you are on. If information is
NOT wanted- and I give it away- I get drained,
FAST.
* My brain struggles to develop questions right
away. I'm not quick witted, but sometimes I am..
yeah, I know..complicated..
* I take A LOT of time to get to know someone.
Like, we are talking, years.. you would be
surprised the people who thought they didn't
know me for years, to find out, 5, 10+ years
later, I became a very important person to them.
It's also vice-versa.
* I care about everyone in my family, including
my husband's family. Every, single, one of them.
* I am a empath. Dream empath to. I can 'sense'
feelings I have no idea where they come from.
Like a 'line' coming to me..Let me meditate,
feel it, process it, then release it.
* That 'super-power'' in my brain is only for
putting information in, not putting it out to
words I speak.
* 100% the time, let me write it. We both will
benefit from that.

* If I need to walk away from any situation due to a negative emotion I feel-let it happen. Again, it'll benefit all of us. You don't want to see me angry.
* Don't let me get angry. That's a very bad thing. It comes on quick. I DONT like that about myself.
* I have lots of trauma I'm currently deep diving, uncovering and recovering from.
* Again, if you want to know, just ask. Don't poke. It'll only provoke.
* If you have patience, I'll be your best friend. For life. I promise.
*I'm 100% faithful. Loyal. Respectful. Honest and Genuine. 100% of the time..to EVERYONE in my life.
*I am 100% all of me, all the time..
and I give all of me-100% of the time..ALWAYS.
*I am a writer, painter, dreamer, gemini, introvert, projector. female. And human. Like me, love me- or don't. Your loss.

This one is for YOU-

It's always been YOU.
It's always been ALL 'for' you.
Since the first time I was standing next to
you..your presence, your energy.. your love..
It's all I've EVER needed and wanted..
Even when I was trying to fight it..
I knew deep down.. it's was YOU!

Then Mira was born..
Then Layla..then Kevin.
I finally had it ALL!
With you!
OUR KIDS are my everything, next you.
Those 3 and you..
Is where magic is born.
It's where love is.
It's what I was searching for my whole life.
It's what I I needed all along..
But it all began..
With YOU.

I've have never known since beauty,
happiness..love..
joy..passion..LIFE, EVER!
I was living life all wrong..

till YOU.

I will always fight for YOU.
For us..
For them. Always.
FOREVER.
I have done it many times before-
And I'll do it over and over again..
All the time..for always..
Till my last breath in this life..
And..Till the end of time.
And that's a promise I'll say over and over
again..
and keep FOREVER.

It's my ONE thing..
You & them.
This love..
Its not just love, but..
UNCONDITIONAL LOVE.
Something I thought,
I didn't deserve..
Till YOU.

A have a SOUL mate in YOU.
A BEST FRIEND.
A partner..a husband.
Who is my BEST friend..
My ONE person..

And he has been since day 1.
And he will always be..
In every lifetime..
For a thousand lifetimes..
He will always be my
EVERYTHING.
Till the end of time..

My love is..
NOT just a deep bond.
Oh no..It's more like,
A set-in-stone kind of thing..
Solid. Concrete.
A FOREVER bond.
That will never be broken.
It may crack, give way.. it may even rip at the
seams..
But it's NEVER broken.
Oh no. For that can NEVER, EVER..
be fully broken.
For love always wins.
It always finds a way.
Every. Single. time.
Love brings light to the darkness.
For even the darkest star, has a little light..
All it has to do.. is shine.

And when that light.. that love,
Starts to show signs of wear and tear..

(As it will, because we are human & that's ok
sometimes)
I'll always strive with every ounce of my body,
heart & soul..
to bring every piece by piece,
back together..
However long that takes..
For whatever that takes.
Blood. Sweat. Tears.
As long as the light of love keeps shine back at
me..
I'll fight to the death to sew it all back together.
Stitch by stitch.
Patch by patch..
But you see.. after every piece makes its way
back together..
All sewn back together in disarray..
It makes what only could be called..
A work of art.
Some may describe it, and judge it as..
A train wreck, mismatched junk or
even a fucking disaster of a tangled mess.
But I would call it..
A design of perfectly imperfect,
beautifully hand crafted..
A beautiful chaos..
patch quilt. Made by us!
For it was made with lovely care.
It has bright colors, like neon pink & green..

It has all shapes & sizes, especially..
Hearts & stars.
It was made with hands covered in dirt &
grime..which made incredible handprints to be
displayed for a lifetime.
But above all..
It was made with..
unconditional love..
It's the art of love.

So, someday..
Many, many years from now..
When I'm much, much older and much more
grey..
When I have fulfilled & accomplished all my
hopes & dreams with YOU..
When I leave this earth and go..
I, 100%, absolutely, without a doubt..
Want to leave this earth..
with you by my side!
And by the time this happens & when it does..
We better be doing some crazy fun shit, LIVING
life, traveling the world over..together!
 Maning OUR dreams come true over & over
again..
And don't forget the wild, carefree road trips &
adventures all mixed in..
I want to be riding (street) motorcycles during
the sunset, somewhere so beautiful..

Only god can take us from it.
We will be going out with a BLAST..together!

And at our celebration of life..
I want family & friends to say..

'Dam.. those two had IT.
They had that love..
That PASSION..
That kind of love that is only in fairy tales.
That so many spend their whole lives trying to
find..but never get to fully experience it.
But dam.. did they LIVE!
They were fucking CRAZY!!
Probably border line, insane..
(Most likely true)
But.. dam..
did they live.. TOGETHER!!
They rode out of this world, doing the shit they
love.. and dam.. what a life they had!'

Go fly away

You say it looks amazing,
But where are you?
You left so long ago..
I barely recognize your touch.
Your face, your voice, your whole demeanor..it's
different..
What happened to you? What happened to us?
I thought we had a soul connection..
A forever bond.. a love that would last a
lifetime..
It's beautiful here, without you..
The sun is rising over the hills..
The birds are singing, the sunlight hitting the
water..The air is crisp, the light clouds,
diminishing..just like you..
It was the first place I took you,
So many years ago.
Long drive, sunsets & sunrises..
So many memories here,
But where are you?
You're so entangled in yourself, you can't see..
You never were like this before..
Always loving, always encouraging,
Always full of life..
I've tried so many times, to keep it alive..

For you. For us.. for them..
But do you even want that anymore?
I feel, every time I try to reach you,
I'm left hanging.. alone..lost..confused &
unloved..
I guess I'm pushing too hard..for you..
to love me..the why I love you..
Im so deeply hurt by your actions & your
words.. they cut deep. Those words, said by
you..
Then the very next day..
'I didn't say that' or 'that's not what I meant'
Well, I'm logical..and so are you, so..
Whatever words come out of your mouth,
Those are the words, that I hear.
So, where are you? Where have you been?
Do you even want to come back to me?
Just two weeks ago, you were in love with me..
all over me, couldn't keep your hands off of me..
couldn't stop you from talking all day & night..
Now, all of a sudden.. no talking, no real deep
connection. Nothing. Just empty..
I long, just see you smile.. to hear you laugh..I
long for you.. are you even in there, anymore?
I long to have that deep connection with
you..those long talks, about our hopes &
dreams..like we always had..
Or, was it that, this whole time,
I just didn't see.. Was I just that blind?

Were you ever happy? Were you ever truly
happy with me?
Or were you just faking it, since we made a
family together..
I never faked it. Never once..I never saw anyone
else, not even for a second..
it was only you. I never wanted anyone else..
You were all I ever needed..
You were always enough..
Evey single day. For 12 years.
Yeah, sure, we had our rough patches..
But we had love… so I thought..
It just doesn't make any sense now,
Why string me out this long? To only, pull the
rug from underneath me? Why let it go this long,
to tell me those words? To tell me, I don't do it
for you anymore.. that I haven't in a long time..
why? That can't be true..
I was so happy. I was so in love. So in love.. so
madly in love with you, every single day..for
years.. but now..
I feel so broken. So lost. So.. without.. you.
So, as I sit here, and watch the sun brush its light
on everything it touches.. I think of you..
I can't help but think..
Where is our light? Where is your light? Where
is mine?
Maybe we lost it long ago.. maybe it's just too
late for any kind of repair..

All I know, is you..
I never wanted anything more..than you.
If I don't have you, to do this life with me..
Then what is this life? Empty. A empty dark
hole.. with no light shining through..
But without you, I will have no choice..
But to going every day..for them.
I will get up every morning, and put on smile on
them..our babies we made together..
Remember that time, I asked you..
'What about the kids, if we don't stay together?'
'Don't you want better than we had, growing
up?'
I wanted nothing more than to give them that.. to
have what I didn't.. parents that loved each
other, for always & forever.. till the end of time..
who stayed together through it all..
I wanted to show them, what a good, healthy
marriage looks like, show them what true love
looks like..but maybe, that's just what I
wanted..and not you..
I wanted them to have that.. that love.. between
their parents..to bring to their future
relationships..
But you replied 'what about the happiness of the
parents?' 'Doesn't that matter?'
I didn't understand what you meant.. or why you
would say that..
Until now..

Maybe you're right..
Maybe, it's the happiness of the parent's that
matters most..
But what about my happiness?
My happiness is with you..
but maybe I'm just being selfish, hoping you
will stay.. maybe I'm being selfish for wanting
you to stay..
but fine. You win..
Go find your happiness. Don't die on
display-like cut flowers, to just enjoy a short
while -don't die of unhappiness.. don't die in
misery with me..
Go be that free bird, I have always loved in you.
Go 'find yourself' then..Go be that. Go be you.
Whatever, that is..without me..
Because, I love you that much..
To set you free..
To set you free of the chains, you bear with me.
I will die of loneliness..sadness..
despair..heart ache.. but you won't.
You'll die the way god intended..
A free bird. A free man..
So go fly away little birdie..
Go fly away..